Boom-a-tuk, boom-a-tuk, boom-a-tuk
Boom-a-tuk, boom-a-tuk, boom-a-tuk

Written by June Stoute

Illustrated by Jehanne Silva-Freimane

In Barbados the British army used some enslaved Africans as musicians. These musicians played European music for the army marches and parties, but made it more African when playing for their own people. One way they did this was by beating a piece of iron. This mixed music is called Tuk.

Most often a Tuk band has two drummers, a penny whistle and a triangle.

Once these bands played in villages throughout the island. Today, they are seen at major festivals or hotels entertaining tourists.

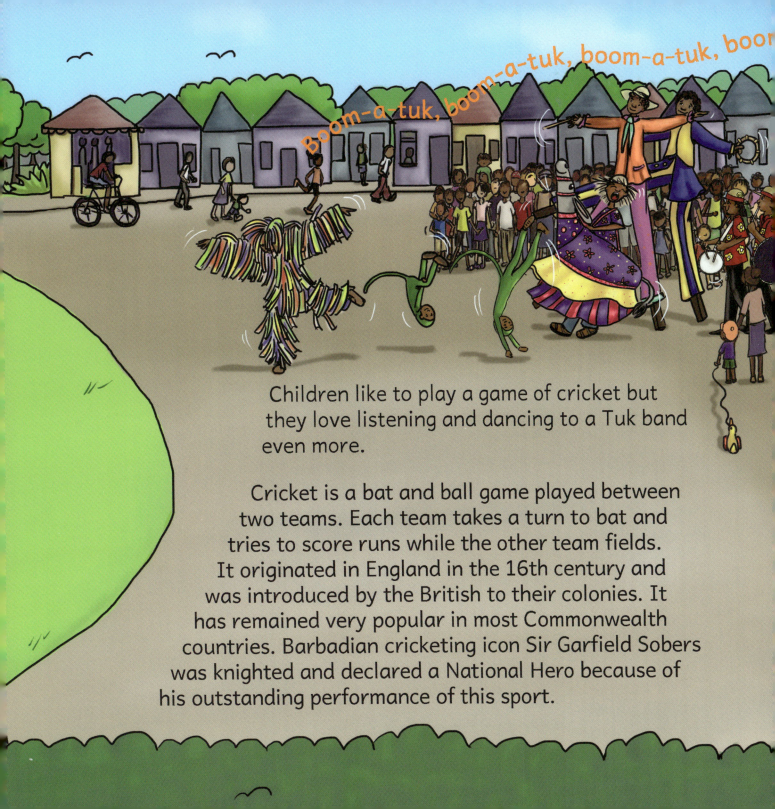

Boom-a-tuk, boom-a-tuk, boom-a-tuk, boom

Children like to play a game of cricket but they love listening and dancing to a Tuk band even more.

Cricket is a bat and ball game played between two teams. Each team takes a turn to bat and tries to score runs while the other team fields. It originated in England in the 16th century and was introduced by the British to their colonies. It has remained very popular in most Commonwealth countries. Barbadian cricketing icon Sir Garfield Sobers was knighted and declared a National Hero because of his outstanding performance of this sport.

Fife and drums of regimental bands –

Since the 14th century, fifes (a type of flute) and drums have been used in the infantry division of European armies. These musicians were called a Corps of Drums. They played a side drum, also called a snare drum, and a fife. The proportions of the side drum changed a lot in the 19th century.

A corps of drums provided music for marching; signaled when it was time to get up or go to bed; when to eat or assemble; sound an alarm; and, during fighting, signaling advance or retreat.

Drummers wore uniforms that were different to that of a soldier. This was to make them easy to see on a battlefield.

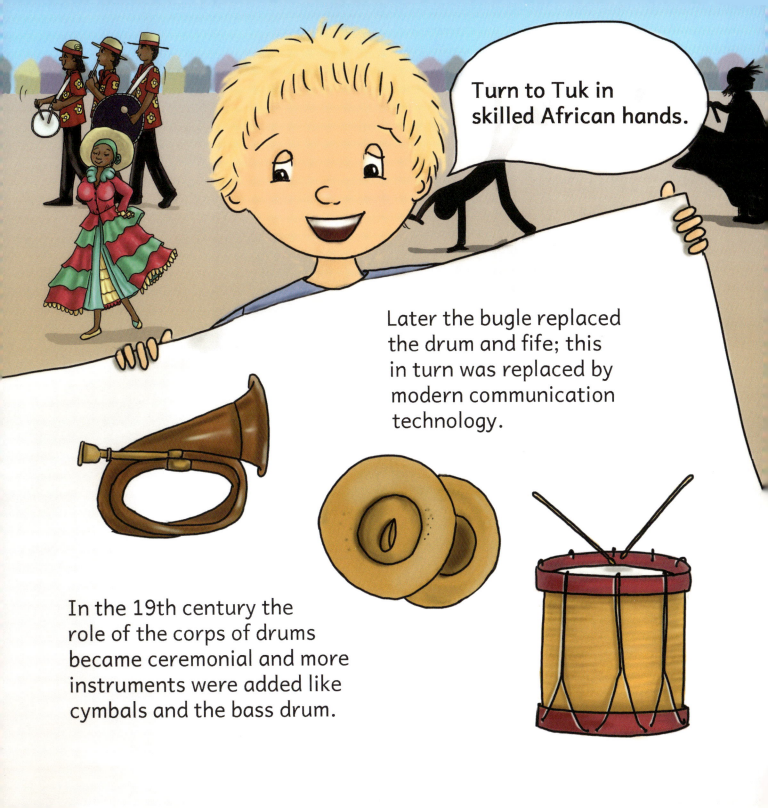

Turn to Tuk in skilled African hands.

Later the bugle replaced the drum and fife; this in turn was replaced by modern communication technology.

In the 19th century the role of the corps of drums became ceremonial and more instruments were added like cymbals and the bass drum.

Drumming is an important part of African life and Africans have many different types of drums. Africans enslaved in Barbados made drums out of materials available locally but in 1688 they were forbidden to play any drums.

Boom-a-tuk, boom-a-tuk, boom-a-tuk, boom

In Tuk two types of drums are used and worn with a diagonal strap over a shoulder. The snare drum is played with two drumsticks.

The bass is played with one drumstick and the musician uses his hand to strike the other side of the drum. The skin of a drum makes a different type of sound when struck by a drumstick than when struck by a hand.

Robert Clarke of Suffolk in England made the first tin whistle in 1843.

The penny or tin whistle plays the tune or melody of the song.
In earlier times, a fiddle was part of a Tuk band and this would play the melody.

The peoples of Africa have played flutes, made of reeds and bamboo, long before their capture and transportation to the *New World*.

"But beware of Shaggy, the raggedy bear. He casts spells as he sails through the air."

The Shaggy Bear is believed to be of African origin as a similar masquerade is worn at the Senegambian yam festivals as well as in other Caribbean islands, but called by different names.

Shaggy does a bouncy, acrobatic dance intended to frighten and amaze. His original costume was made of dried banana leaves, which rustled as he danced and spun, and his face was masked. Some say he is a witch doctor.

Today he is very glamorous in his costume of strips of brightly coloured fabric.

In earlier times, singers and costumed dancers would accompany Tuk bands when they played in Barbadian villages.

At first all the dancers were men and they always wore masks. This was in keeping with the spiritual side of the West African masquerade and the tradition of concealing the flesh to hide the fact that the wearer was human.

Nowadays, singers no longer accompany the bands, both men and women dance but they do not wear masks. In 1960 the Government of Barbados passed a law banning the wearing of masks on roads or in other public places.

Mother Sally, with her supersized bosom and buttocks, is said to be a symbol of the fertility of African women. A masked man wearing women's clothing originally played this masquerade. Today, unmasked women play it. Mother Sally's dance includes vigorous pelvic thrusting and shimmying.

There are similar masquerades in the Gelede Masquerades of Yoruba in Nigeria, in masquerade of the Ga ethnic peoples of Ghana, and in other islands throughout the Caribbean.

Signs that Africans wore masks date back to the Stone Age. Masking was part of the spiritual practices and used for important occasions such as making war, driving out demons and ensuring a good harvest. Very little was written about the practices of the enslaved Africans and so the meaning behind their various masquerades has been lost. Enslaved Africans were taken from the west coast of Africa from Senegal in the north to Angola in the south. As a result, in the Caribbean, there are influences of the culture of many different peoples of Africa and their practices.

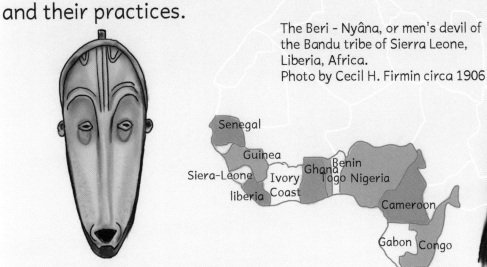

The Beri - Nyâna, or men's devil of the Bandu tribe of Sierra Leone, Liberia, Africa.
Photo by Cecil H. Firmin circa 1906

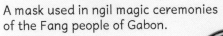

A mask used in ngil magic ceremonies of the Fang people of Gabon.

Kifwebe Sorcerer Dancer, of the Luba people of the Democratic Republic of the Congo.
Photo by Reverend -Father Colle circa 1913

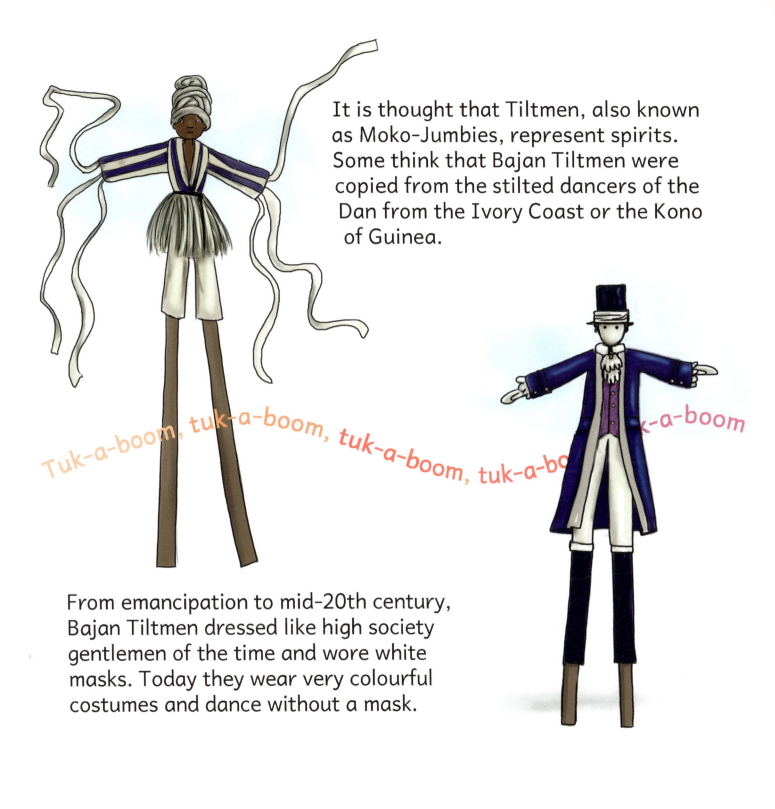

It is thought that Tiltmen, also known as Moko-Jumbies, represent spirits. Some think that Bajan Tiltmen were copied from the stilted dancers of the Dan from the Ivory Coast or the Kono of Guinea.

Tuk-a-boom, tuk-a-boom, tuk-a-boom, tuk-a-boom, tuk-a-boom

From emancipation to mid-20th century, Bajan Tiltmen dressed like high society gentlemen of the time and wore white masks. Today they wear very colourful costumes and dance without a mask.

"Stubborn and strong and dancing this role Donkey represents the resistance of old."

The donkey is the offspring of the African wild ass. Proof that these animals lived in Africa goes back to 4500 BC. West Africans would have known about donkeys before they were captured and carried to Barbados.

Christopher Columbus first brought donkeys to the Americas in the 15th Century.

In the Donkey Man masquerade, the dancer rides a gaily-decorated frame representing a donkey. The head is in front of the dancer and seen from the side it looks like a two-legged animal. It is somewhat like a European hobbyhorse that depicted a knight on an armoured horse.

Stepping high he prances around showing that he does not want to be mounted. He also gallops around in a circle in front of the musicians.

It is thought that this masquerade was played because donkeys were very important to the work done in the sugar cane industry. There were many donkeys in Barbados before machines were used for moving and grinding canes. The donkey, though, is also known to be stubborn and strong-minded.

Today, the Donkey Man masquerade, like the donkey, is rarely seen.

The Green Monkey, a new masquerade, joined the dancers in the late 1990s. It represents the local monkeys that can be seen on the roads and trees throughout Barbados. Its dance is very lively as it copies how the monkeys swing and jump.

The green monkey (Chlorocebus sabaeus) is an old world monkey with golden-green fur and pale hands and feet. The tip of the tail is golden yellow as are the backs of the thighs and cheek whiskers.
(WIKI)

First found in West Africa from Senegal to the Volta River, the green monkey was introduced into the Cape Verde islands, St. Kitts, Nevis, St. Martin and Barbados during the 17th century when slave trade ships sailed to the Caribbean from West Africa.

Senegal
Guinea
Siera-Leone
liberia
Ivory Coast
Ghana
Nigeria
↑
Volta river

Boom-a-tuk, boom-a-tuk, boom-a-tuk, boom boom-a-tuk

Traditionally, there were two types of British army bands. The larger military bands included instruments such as brass and woodwind and played for military reviews, public and troop entertainment, or special events. The smaller "corps of drums", composed of fifes and drums, played field music (music to direct the troops). Tuk grew from this using their instruments and its own rhythms.

Wordways Caribbean promotes Caribbean authors and illustrators who celebrate through their art Caribbean topics and the Caribbean way of life.

Our children's series is designed to entertain young readers while introducing them to aspects of the Caribbean culture. These lively stories are supported by colourful illustrations and amazing facts that will encourage their reading skills while they have fun learning.

© June Stoute 2015
First published 2015
All rights reserved.
Published by Wordways Caribbean,
Prior Park, St. James, Barbados.

ISBN 978-976-95377-4-3

Dear Reader,

After I decided to write this book, I set out to learn everything I could about Tuk. Since childhood, I had seen Tuk bands but this was not enough knowledge to write a book. I visited libraries, web sites and read books written by authors who had done research on Tuk and other subjects I planned to include.

Among the books I read were the Dictionary of Caribbean English Usage by Richard Allsopp (1966) and The Jumbies' Playing Ground by Robert Wyndham Nicholls (2012). In the Journals of the Barbados Museum and Historical Society I read "Treat to Labourers: Plantation Crop Over from Slavery to Independence" (Vol. LVII) by Marcia Burrowes (2011); in Volume LI Sharon Meredith's (2005) Tuk: Origins, Influences and Practices in Colonial Barbados.

On the web at www.rebirth.co.za I found an article called African Masks History and Meaning; at www.ijih.org there was an article by Marcia Burrowes (2011) titled Losing our Masks: Traditional Masquerade and Changing Constructs of Barbadian Identity International (Journal of Intangible Heritage, Vol. 8.). At www.academia.edu I read Roger Blench's The History and Spread of Donkeys in Africa and at www.clothestellstories.com, Folk Culture and Costume at the Folk Museum in Barbados by Allison Callendar.

Wikipedia and Encyclopaedia Britannia were founts of information relating to drums and military bands.

Finally, at www.stjohnhistoricalsociety.org, I came upon Masquerade - Costumes of the Atlantic Rim by Robert W. Nicholls.

The uniforms worn by the British soldiers stationed in Barbados changed from time to time and indeed varied between regiments. The uniforms shown in this book do not represent a specific historical regiment but are based on historical images.

I had fun and learnt a lot writing this book. I hope you do too reading it.

June Stoute

Boom-a-tuk, boom-a-tuk, boom-a-tuk, boom-a-tuk, boom

Find the hidden words in the puzzle.

```
A M F Y A Z Y S O L D I E R O R D Q
O A T C J B T B A N D C R T I Q A U
R S I M D A Y D J N R F Z H K M N M
M K L U O F W R E T E G B T S A C O
O B T S N R H U F F G D F M I L E N
T W M I K I I M R I I Y I E N L U K
C D A C E C S T L D M E A L G E L E
T N N I Y A T D K D E L R O E T J Y
O H G A L N L S F L N W M D R O D Q
U F H N H M E Z Z E T R Y Y S R C I
K A W S V T V Z S H A G G Y W I H U
Y N D L I B N O Y Y U F I F E J S G
```

AFRICAN	FIFE	SHAGGY
ARMY	MALLET	SINGERS
BAND	MASK	SOLDIER
DANCE	MELODY	TILTMAN
DONKEY	MONKEY	TOUK
DRUM	MUSICIANS	WHISTLE
FIDDLE	REGIMENT	

More books for you to enjoy.

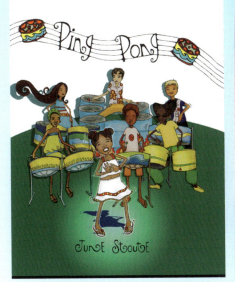
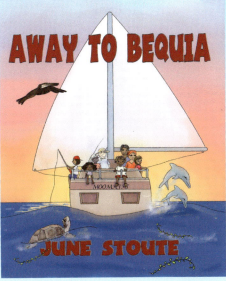
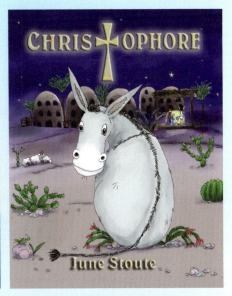
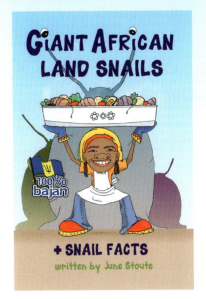
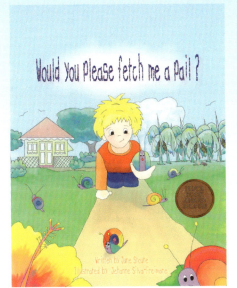
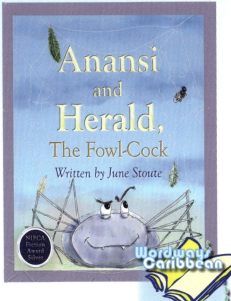

CPSIA information can be obtained at www.ICGtesting.com
Printed in the USA
LVIW01n0527150415
434455LV00004B/18